JENNIE MAIZELS

STICKER ACTIVITY

LONDON

WALKER BOOKS
AND SUBSIDIARIES

LONDON • BOSTON • SYDNEY • AUCKLAND

Buckingham Palace

Buckingham Palace became the official London residence of the Royal Family after Queen Victoria's coronation in 1837. When the monarch is in residence, the flag that flies is the Royal Standard.

The famous Changing of the Guard ceremony takes place at 11.30 a.m. each day. Use the stickers to finish this marching scene.

Fun Facts

Built: 1703–1913

Located: At the end of The Mall.

Famous for: Being the official residence of the UK's monarch.

Did You Know?: The palace has 775 different rooms with 19 lavish state rooms!

Can you untangle the wires to find out who is calling the Queen?

Buckingham Palace receives more than 700,000 telephone calls a year.

Hello?

1

2

3

There's so much to see at Buckingham Palace. Complete the picture crossword.

5

6

4

7

8

The palace garden is the oldest helicopter pad in London – it was first used in 1953, just before Queen Elizabeth II's coronation.

Spot the difference! Can you find six differences between these pictures?

The Tower of London

The Tower was once a prison and place of execution. Anne Boleyn, wife of Henry VIII, was executed on Tower Green, as was Lady Jane Grey. The famous White Tower, built by William the Conqueror between 1075 and 1101, is the oldest intact building in London.

The Ceremony of the Keys, in which the Tower is locked up at night, is the oldest military ceremony in the world – unchanged for over 700 years.

During the 1200s a royal zoo was founded at the Tower. It housed exotic animals like lions and polar bears for over 600 years!

Fun Facts

Built: 11–15th century

Located: On the banks of the River Thames.

Famous for: Being home to the magnificent Crown Jewels.

Did You Know?: The Beefeaters who guard the Tower of London are officially called "Yeoman Warders".

Complete the sentences below by reading all the clues on this page.

1. _ _ _ _ Boleyn was executed at the Tower.

2. Centuries ago, you could see exotic _ _ _ _ _ _ _ here.

3. The Tower was built by William the _ _ _ _ _ _ _ _ _ _ .

4. A guard of the Tower is called a _ _ _ _ _ _ _ _ _ _ _ _ _ .

5. The _ _ _ _ _ _ _ _ _ _ _ are associated with the Royal Family.

6. The Ceremony of the _ _ _ _ has existed for over 700 years.

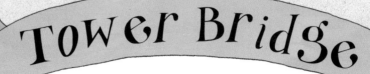
Tower Bridge

One of the most famous bridges in the world, Tower Bridge can open to allow tall ships to pass through. Through glass panels on the upper walkway you can see traffic on the bridge below.

Fun Facts

Built: 1886–1894

Located:
Spanning the River Thames.

Famous for:
Opening when tall ships need to pass underneath.

Did You Know?:
The bridge opens to let ships pass about 850 times per year.

Use your stickers to build Tower Bridge.

In 1912, a daredevil pilot flew his aeroplane between the lower and upper parts of the bridge.

Ships always take priority. In 1997, the American president had to wait in his car whilst a sailing barge passed through.

Open Sesame!

Houses of Parliament

England's first official parliament was established at the Palace of Westminster in 1295. Politicians meet here daily to discuss the way Britain is governed and to make laws.

The famous Palace of Westminster we know today was constructed after an enormous fire in 1834 destroyed most of the earlier government buildings.

The oldest building in the current Houses of Parliament complex is Westminster Hall, built in 1097 and originally used for administration and legal judgements.

Fun Facts

Built: 1840–1870

Located: Westminster

Famous for: Being the home of the UK parliament.

Did You Know?
Parliament is made up of two parts: the House of Commons and the House of Lords.

Tick, tock

Read all the facts, then find a sticker at the back of the book to match each one.

1. The House of Commons has green seats and its politicians are elected by public vote.

2. Big Ben is actually the nickname of the bell inside the famous clock tower, which is called the Elizabeth Tower.

3. The House of Lords has red seats. Most of its members are chosen by politicians.

There have been lawmakers in London for centuries – and some ancient laws, even though they seem very strange today, are still in place.

Can you guess whether each of the laws below is real or not?

It is illegal...

1. to enter the Houses of Parliament wearing a suit of armour. **True** ❏ / **False** ❏

2. to place a stamp of the Queen upside down on a letter. **True** ❏ / **False** ❏

3. to beat or shake a doormat in the street – except before 8 a. m. **True** ❏ / **False** ❏

4. to carry a plank along a pavement. **True** ❏ / **False** ❏

5. to die in Parliament. **True** ❏ / **False** ❏

6. to fire cannon within 275 metres of a house. **True** ❏ / **False** ❏

7. to drive cattle through the streets – unless the Commissioner of Police gives his approval. **True** ❏ / **False** ❏

8. to crack a boiled egg at the pointed end. **True** ❏ / **False** ❏

9. for a lady to eat chocolate on public transport. **True** ❏ / **False** ❏

10. to handle salmon in suspicious circumstances. **True** ❏ / **False** ❏

Guy Fawkes tried to blow up Parliament with barrels of gunpowder on 5 November 1605, but was caught and executed.

Haunted London

London is often said to be the most haunted capital in the world, with ghosts that span the centuries. Established in AD 43 by the Romans, the city has witnessed 2,000 years of human history. Perhaps ghosts still linger in London today, appearing in places of great happiness or misery...

Each of the spooky stories below has a matching sticker. Can you put them all in the right place?

1. Every Christmas Day, a ghost comes to Buckingham Palace. A monastery once stood where the palace is now, and a monk who starved to death there makes a haunting appearance each year.

2. Father Benedictus, a friendly monk, haunts the cloisters of Westminster Abbey. He once entertained a group of tourists for nearly half an hour!

3. Many visitors to St Paul's Cathedral have reported a whistling old man disappearing through a wall. During renovation after World War One, a hidden door was found in the spot the whistler visits, leading to a secret room.

4. The West London neighbourhood of Ladbroke Grove is home to a phantom double-decker bus which has been known to appear suddenly, terrifying drivers and sometimes causing fatal crashes.

St Paul's Cathedral

St Paul's Cathedral is one of London's most recognizable landmarks with its famous dome and enormous crypt, the largest in Europe. Inside the dome is the Whispering Gallery, where a whisper on one side can be heard 30 metres away on the other.

Lord Nelson, who led the English to victory at the Battle of Trafalgar, is buried in the crypt. His body was transported home in a wooden barrel filled with brandy and wine!

Use your stickers to build the cathedral.

Fun Facts

Built: 1675–1700

Located: At the highest point in the City of London.

Famous for: Its huge dome, within which lies the mysterious Whispering Gallery.

Did You Know?: It was designed by Sir Christopher Wren after the previous building was destroyed in the Great Fire.

The Great Fire of London was an enormous fire that swept through central London in 1666 after starting at a bakery. The homes of 70,000 people were destroyed.

Natural History Museum

The Natural History Museum has thousands of specimens of plants and animals, both living and extinct. It is most famous for its dinosaur exhibits, including huge skeletons and life-size dinosaur robots that give you an insight into the prehistoric era.

Use your stickers to complete this jigsaw of the blue whale model.

Use your stickers to build the famous skeleton of Diplodocus.

My name's Dippy. I'm actually a replica made of plaster. I have 292 separate bones!

Find the words below. They can run forwards, backwards, up and down!

E	A	R	T	H	Q	U	A	K	E	A	J
T	C	V	H	H	B	R	Y	X	N	H	Q
E	I	H	H	C	L	C	Q	V	T	E	G
K	R	O	I	N	K	N	R	F	E	X	Q
C	O	Z	S	M	T	O	U	A	Y	H	E
I	T	A	T	H	R	T	A	B	G	I	R
T	S	N	O	W	E	E	S	G	O	B	U
R	I	I	R	H	E	L	O	X	L	I	T
G	H	M	Y	A	E	E	N	B	O	T	A
R	E	A	I	L	I	K	I	W	E	I	N
E	R	L	W	E	C	S	D	L	G	O	X
D	P	B	W	M	U	S	E	U	M	N	W

ANIMAL
DINOSAUR
EARTHQUAKE
EXHIBITION
GEOLOGY
HISTORY
MUSEUM
NATURE
PREHISTORIC
SKELETON
TICKET
TREE
WHALE

At 26 metres long, Diplodocus is one of the largest animals ever to have walked on earth.

Fun Facts

Opened: 1881

Located: South Kensington

Famous for: Celebrating the natural world.

Did You Know?: Hidden inside the belly of the museum's enormous blue whale model lies a telephone directory from the 1930s!

The Natural History Museum is in an area known as "Museum District". Nearby are the Science Museum and the artsy Victoria & Albert Museum.

Famous Shops

London's shops have something for everyone. Visitors can disappear into the crowds of Oxford Street, stroll along elegant Regent Street, or window shop in extravagant Knightsbridge.

1. Hamleys

This gigantic toy shop has been enchanting children since 1881 with seven play-filled floors.

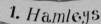

?

Use your stickers to match the shop to the kind of things you can buy there.

2. Selfridges

The largest shop on Oxford Street, this enormous department store contains 100,000 pairs of women's shoes.

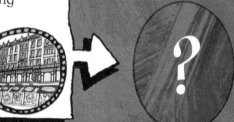

?

Fun Facts

HARRODS

Built: 1894–1905

Located: Knightsbridge

Famous For: Selling deluxe merchandise.

Did You Know?
Harrods used to have a zoo department that sold elephants, alligators and lions!

3. Harrods

The Harrods motto is "everything for everybody, everywhere", which explains why it has 330 different departments!

?

Tate Modern

Housed in a former power station, the Tate Modern is the world's most popular modern art gallery. The huge Turbine Hall, which once contained electricity generators, now displays large, specially commissioned artworks.

Op art is usually black and white. It uses optical illusions, tricking the viewer into thinking the art is moving, flashing or contains hidden images.

Put your stickers in the right place to copy this piece of op art. Be careful – it's tricky!

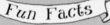

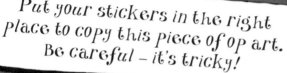

The distinctive building was constructed using approximately 4.2 million bricks!

See a Show

There's always something going on in London. You can watch performances both in famous theatres and on the city streets, attend sports events at the Olympic stadium, or a rock concert at an enormous arena.

There are 18,000 theatre performances in London each year, attended by almost 14 million people!

Can you place the stickers correctly to complete this picture sudoku? Each row and each column should contain one of the buildings below – but never more than one!

Royal Albert Hall
A spectacular building used for concerts, award ceremonies and exhibitions.

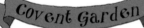
Covent Garden
Home to street entertainers, shops and a renowned opera house.

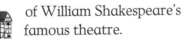
The Globe
A faithful reconstruction of William Shakespeare's famous theatre.

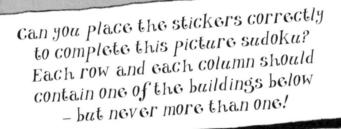

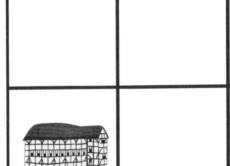

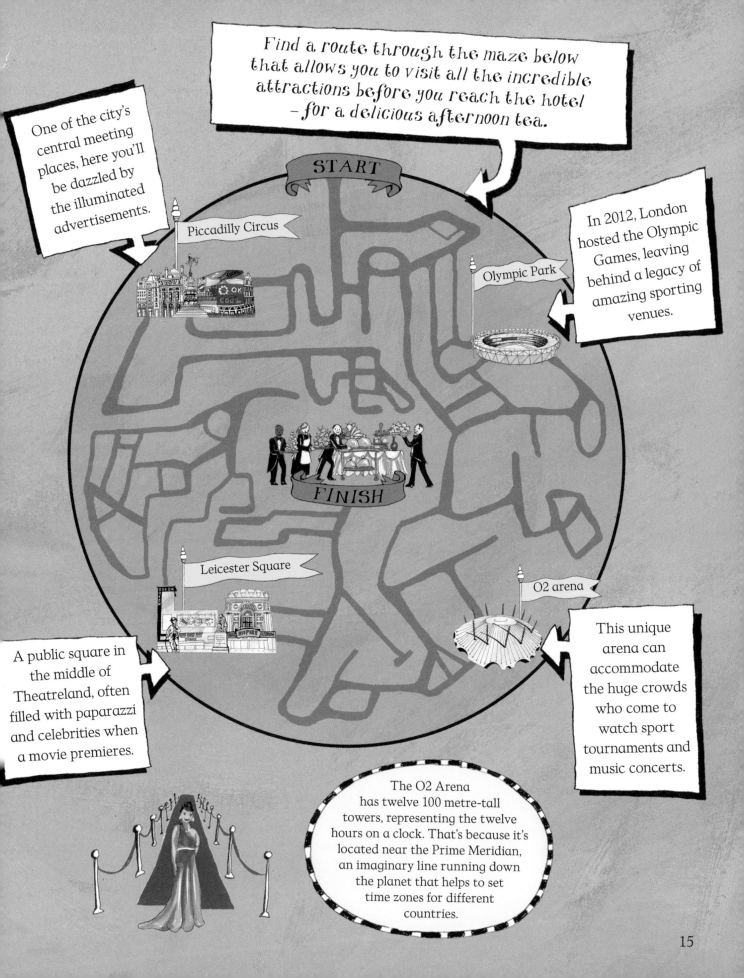

Find a route through the maze below that allows you to visit all the incredible attractions before you reach the hotel – for a delicious afternoon tea.

START

One of the city's central meeting places, here you'll be dazzled by the illuminated advertisements.

Piccadilly Circus

In 2012, London hosted the Olympic Games, leaving behind a legacy of amazing sporting venues.

Olympic Park

FINISH

Leicester Square

O2 arena

A public square in the middle of Theatreland, often filled with paparazzi and celebrities when a movie premieres.

This unique arena can accommodate the huge crowds who come to watch sport tournaments and music concerts.

The O2 Arena has twelve 100 metre-tall towers, representing the twelve hours on a clock. That's because it's located near the Prime Meridian, an imaginary line running down the planet that helps to set time zones for different countries.

The London Eye

The world's tallest observation wheel was built to celebrate the new millennium. It takes 30 minutes to rotate at a relaxed speed of 26 cm per second – that's twice as fast as a tortoise sprinting.

The London Eye is the star of a breathtaking firework display every New Year's Eve – use your stickers to fill the sky with colourful explosions!

Fun Facts

Opened: 2000

Located: On the south bank of the River Thames.

Famous for: Providing spectacular views of London.

Did You Know?: The London Eye is 135 metres tall – that's as high as 64 red telephone boxes piled on top of one another!

Here are five of the wheel's capsules. Match the pairs and find the odd one out.

Parks and Gardens

London has eight Royal Parks, which are filled with places for picnics, playing sports and even watching films on a big screen. The Royal Botanic Gardens at Kew are home to the largest collection of plants on the planet!

Hyde Park is London's most famous park. It includes the Serpentine Lake, Speaker's Corner and the Diana, Princess of Wales Memorial Fountain.

Kew Gardens isn't just filled with plants – it's also teeming with animal life! There are over 20 badger setts, as well as a bee garden and a marine aquarium.

Can you find all the words in the list below? Words run up, down, forwards, backwards and diagonally.

Y	H	E	L	I	C	U	F	E	D	Y	H
N	G	K	E	L	N	L	C	W	N	L	R
A	W	A	A	S	O	C	A	F	O	B	Y
T	E	L	V	W	M	I	K	J	P	U	S
O	K	I	E	P	L	N	B	O	B	K	N
B	A	R	S	A	K	C	M	G	E	R	E
T	S	V	Y	J	F	I	B	G	N	A	D
W	M	O	V	Y	B	P	N	I	C	P	R
G	R	E	E	N	E	R	Y	N	H	I	A
X	V	I	O	V	K	X	Z	G	X	W	G
L	E	S	U	O	H	N	E	E	R	G	Q
Z	F	R	I	S	B	E	E	I	I	P	H

BENCH
BOTANY
FLOWERS
FRISBEE
GARDENS
GREENERY
GREENHOUSE
HYDE
JOGGING
KEW
LAKE
LEAVES
PARK
PICNIC
POND
ROYAL

Getting Around Town

Keeping London moving requires a number of different means of transport. You can jump aboard a famous double-decker bus, descend into the Tube, the world's oldest underground railway network, hop in a black cab, and even travel by boat down the River Thames!

Every licensed taxi driver must pass a famous test called "The Knowledge". That means remembering 25,000 streets and 20,000 landmarks – yikes!

Can you spot eight differences between these two London buses?

After World War One, a shortage of London buses led some enterprising people to start unofficial bus services known as "pirate buses". Races between the pirate and proper buses became common, terrifying passengers!

Three babies have been born on the London Underground, most recently a boy born in 2009.

Where are these taxis going?
Untangle the routes to find out who's visiting which destination, then find the matching sticker.

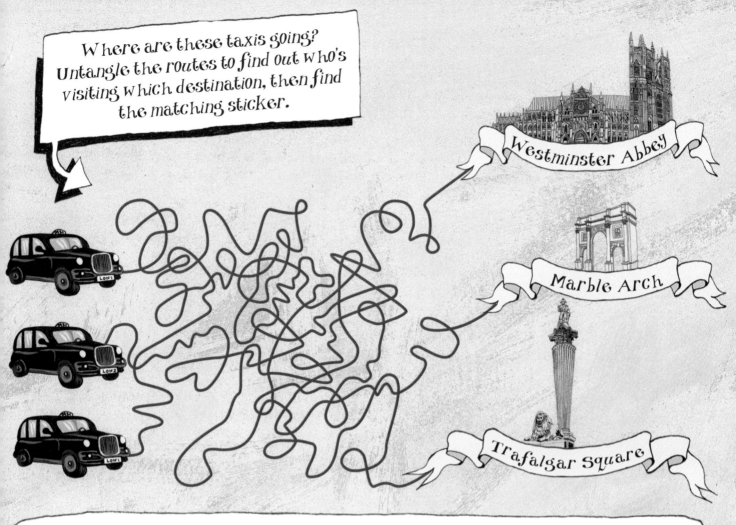

Westminster Abbey

Marble Arch

Trafalgar Square

Can you find the correct boat stickers to complete the sentences below?

1. The  patrols the Thames, helping to fight crime and keep people safe.

2. If you want to explore London by both land and water, take a trip on the  .

3. Thousands of people go to work each day on the  , a large passenger boat.

4. The  is part of a world-famous rowing race between two ancient universities.

London

London is an enormous sprawling capital. "The City of London" refers to the square mile originally settled by the Romans. The rest of London is made up of 32 separate boroughs, each with its own distinctive character.

WESTMINST

KENSINGTON & CHELSEA

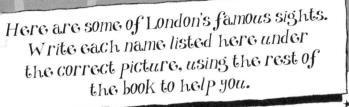

Here are some of London's famous sights. Write each name listed here under the correct picture, using the rest of the book to help you.

- ★ Buckingham Palace
- ★ St Paul's Cathedral
- ★ Shakespeare's Globe
- ★ Houses of Parliament
- ★ Hamleys

- ★ The City
- ★ Natural History Museum
- ★ Royal Albert Hall
- ★ Selfridges
- ★ Tower of London
- ★ Tower Bridge

- ★ Tate Modern
- ★ Trafalgar Square
- ★ Harrods
- ★ Covent Garden
- ★ British Museum
- ★ London Eye

CAMDEN

SOUTHWARK

RIVER THAMES

LAMBETH

Answers

Page 2

Page 3 Crossword:
1. Guard
2. Carriage
3. Bed
4. Corgi
5. Palace
6. Curtains
7. Piano
8. Footman

Page 4
1. Anne
2. animals
3. 1066
4. Yeoman Warder
5. Crown Jewels
6. Keys

Page 7
1.   2.   3.

It is illegal . . .
1. True   6. True
2. False   7. True
3. True   8. False
4. True   9. False
5. False   10. True

Page 8
1.   2.   3.   4.

Page 10

Page 11

E	A	R	T	H	Q	U	A	K	E	A	J
T	C	V	H	H	B	R	Y	X	N	H	Q
E	I	H	H	C	L	C	Q	V	T	E	G
K	R	O	I	N	K	N	R	F	E	X	Q
C	O	Z	S	M	T	O	U	A	B	G	E
I	T	A	T	H	R	E	A	B	G	O	R
T	S	N	O	I	W	E	L	G	O	L	U
R	I	I	R	H	H	E	E	X	L	I	T
G	H	M	Y	A	E	E	N	B	O	T	I
R	E	A	L	I	L	I	K	I	W	E	O
E	R	L	W	E	E	C	S	D	L	G	N
D	P	B	W	M	U	S	E	U	M	N	X

Page 12
1.   2.   3.

Page 13

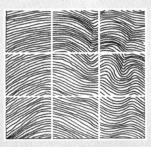

Page 14

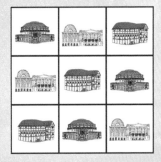

Page 15

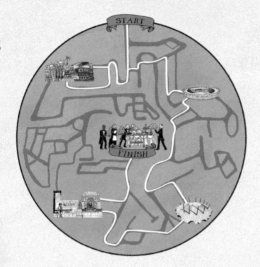

START

FINISH

Page 16

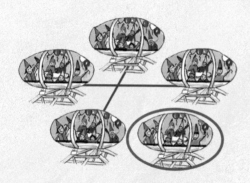

Page 17

Y	H	E	L	I	C	U	F	E	D	Y	H
N	G	K	E	L	N	I	C	W	N	L	R
A	W	A	A	S	O	C	A	F	O	B	Y
T	E	L	V	W	M	I	K	J	P	U	S
O	K	I	E	P	I	N	B	O	B	K	N
B	A	R	S	A	K	C	M	G	E	R	E
T	S	V	Y	J	F	I	B	G	N	A	D
W	M	O	V	Y	B	P	N	I	C	P	R
G	R	E	E	N	E	R	Y	N	H	I	A
X	V	I	O	V	K	X	Z	G	X	W	G
L	E	S	U	O	H	N	E	E	R	G	Q
Z	F	R	I	S	B	E	E	I	I	P	H

Page 18

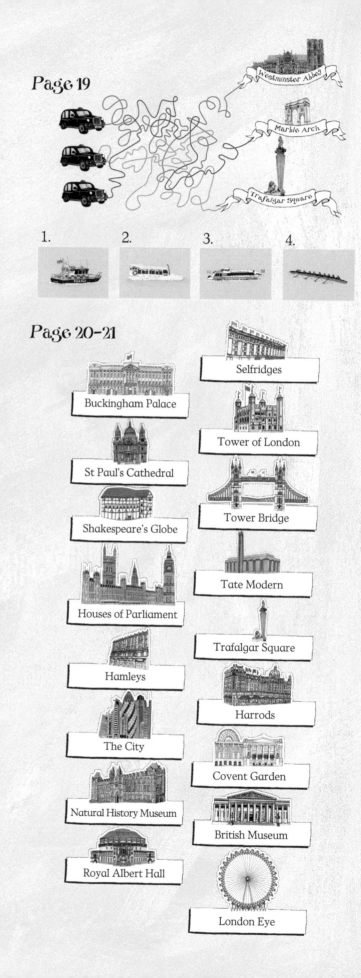

The world of JENNIE MAIZELS

ISBN 978-1-4063-2157-9

ISBN 978-1-4063-6426-2

ISBN 978-1-4063-4945-0

First published 2015 by Walker Books Ltd
87 Vauxhall Walk, London SE11 5HJ

2 4 6 8 10 9 7 5 3 1

Text © 2015 Walker Books Ltd. Illustrations © 2011 Jennie Maizels

The right of Jennie Maizels to be identified as illustrator of this work has been asserted by her in accordance
with the Copyright, Designs and Patents Act 1988

This book has been typeset in Veronan and hand-lettered by Jennie Maizels

Printed in China

British Library Cataloguing in Publication Data: a catalogue record for this book is available from the British Library

ISBN 978-1-4063-6427-9

www.walker.co.uk

Page 2.

Page 5.

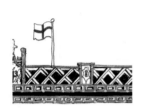   

Page 7.

Page 8.

Page 9.

Page 10.

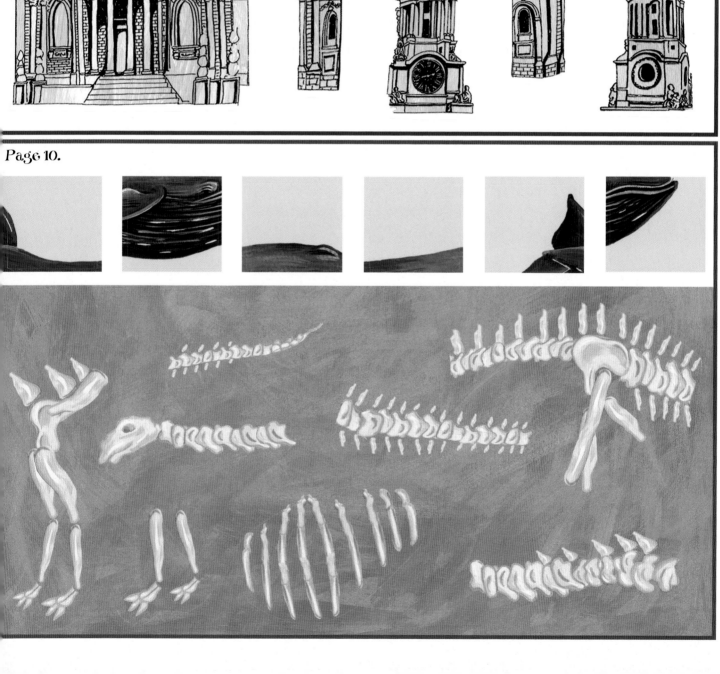

Page 12.

  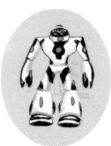

Page 13.

Page 14.

Page 16.

Page 19.